BEYOND THE FLAMES

ESSENTIAL TRANSLATIONS SERIES 19

**Canada Council
for the Arts**

**Conseil des Arts
du Canada**

ONTARIO ARTS COUNCIL
CONSEIL DES ARTS DE L'ONTARIO

50 YEARS OF ONTARIO GOVERNMENT SUPPORT OF THE ARTS
50 ANS DE SOUTIEN DU GOUVERNEMENT DE L'ONTARIO AUX ARTS

Guernica Editions Inc. acknowledges the support of the Canada Council
for the Arts and the Ontario Arts Council.
The Ontario Arts Council is an agency of the Government of Ontario.
We acknowledge the financial support of the Government of Canada
through the National Translation Program for Book Publishing
for our translation activities.
We acknowledge the financial support of the Government of Canada
through the Canada Book Fund (CBF) for our publishing activities.

LOUISE DUPRÉ

BEYOND
THE FLAMES

Translated from the French
by Antonio D'Alfonso

GUERNICA
TORONTO · BUFFALO · LANCASTER (U.K.)
2014

Original title: *Plus haut que les flammes* (Éditions du Noroît, 2010)

Michael Mirolla, Editor
Guernica Editions Inc.
P.O. Box 76080, Abbey Market, Oakville, (ON), Canada L6M 3H5
2250 Military Road, Tonawanda, N.Y. 14150-6000 U.S.A.

Typesetting by Antonio D'Alfonso

Distributors:
University of Toronto Press Distribution,
5201 Dufferin Street, Toronto, (ON), Canada M3H 5T8
Gazelle Book Services, White Cross Mills, High Town, Lancaster LA1 4XS U.K.
First edition.
Printed in Canada.

Legal Deposit – First Quarter
National Library of Canada
Library of Congress Catalog Card Number: 2013950994
Library and Archives Canada Cataloguing in Publication
Dupré, Louise, 1949-
[Plus haut que les flammes. English]
Beyond the flames / Louise Dupré ; Antonio D'Alfonso, translator.
(Essential translations series ; 19)
Translation of: Plus haut que les flammes.
Poems.
Issued in print and electronic formats.
ISBN 978-1-55071-855-3 (pbk.). — ISBN 978-1-55071-856-0 (epub). —
ISBN 978-1-55071-857-7 (mobi)
I. D'Alfonso, Antonio, 1953-, translator II. Title. III. Title: Plus
haut que les flammes. English. IV. Series: Essential translations series ; 19
PS8557.U66P5813 2014   C841'.54   C2013-906664-0
                                                 C2013-906665-9

CONTENTS

To Maxime,
the child
beside me

I

I said, I can take no more
evil in the world.

Claude Esteban

Your poem rose
from hell

one morning as words surprised you
paralyzed
in the middle of a verse

a hell of images
rummaging in the ashes
of furnaces

and souls
without recourse
taking cover inside your mind

it happened after that trip
you came back from

eyes burned to the quick
for seeing nothing

nothing
but remains

as if speaking
of an urn
at a wake

a time for meditation
in front of shovelfuls of earth

because life blossoms
even in the most
uninhabitable of soils

life is life

and we learn to fit
Auschwitz or Birkenau
in a verse

like an unbearable
breath

you must not allow despair
to widen the holes
in your heart

you are not alone

beside you
stands a child

who breaks down
crying

and you want to see him
laugh
out of these tears

you need laughter
to start the morning right

and you find happiness
as in gymnastics

by stretching your arms
towards the branches of a maple tree
outside your window

when a swallow calls out to
springtime

here is this child
you were not waiting for

born
with bronchial tubes
far too narrow to contain light

a child ushered by grief
like a story
void of mercy

you watch him
playing with a flock of clouds
inside a cotton book

and think
about the small-size clothes
belonging to children in Auschwitz

in Auschwitz
where they exterminated children

who played with
flocks of clouds

their coats and dresses small
and this broken feeding bottle
in the window

poverty of memory
for lack of coffins

and tourists
in serried ranks
under fluorescent lights

as you stand waiting

your back bent over
as though everyone on earth
were suddenly leaning on your shoulders

there are feeding bottles breaking

children in Auschwitz
were children
whose mouths gasped with thirst

and the child
beside you

is hungry and thirsty
and you keep your promises
by the armful

if only all depended on you

but here is the world
and its madness

stench of raw blood
and dogs running
after their prey

even when you
find happiness
as in gymnastics

or during a prayer
without hope

there are prayers
for women
without hope

prayers whispered in a voice
woven with adversity
inspiration for books

because the earth has welcomed
more disasters
than blessings

fire
or rain of insects

rock rain
with which to stone wives

shell rain
thrown on cities
like eggs

rain of rain that always
engulfs everything

luckily there are arches
for women
without hope

and for young boys
tall as clouds

crossing over
their first dreams

summer after summer
when pagan laughter
ricochets off eyes

fairground days
on merry-go-rounds

that wave the white
ghost of God

because God is a memory
for Low Mass

no one
will pity
you here

neither this world nor the shrouds
that furrow the sky
like faces

you belong to the muddy
earth

of sepulchers
and animals

you cannot hear the cry
of knives

you used to feed yourself
back when you lived in caves
where you sheltered your children

before you learned to stand
on two feet

stand, as you now stand
straight

with this child beside you
who imitates your gestures

who is unaware of the slaughterhouses
and torture

you remind him that he must eat

as you yourself begin to eat
with your milk teeth

life begins
with a jaw

and beef hanging
on hooks at the market

you remember the blue dress
your mother wore on Friday

and your hand humid in hers
that you must not let go

like those children
in Birkenau seen in photographs

snapped before the wrenching started

their screams smothered
still haunt
the fields

like a wind
of death

there is shame
there are mothers too
whose hearts burst

the heart is not an abstract notion

the heart is a mechanism
of silence
a cornucopia

in which one collects
grief

in rooms, children
wavering between syllables

pasted
on the walls of bronchial tubes
before they collapse

and soldiers every single day
and the imperative patience

ovens to feed
ovens to clean

turning on the oven
you are afraid

for the child beside you
hungry like the horizon

without telling him
about Auschwitz or Birkenau

there are stories
you cannot tell
him

you don't want to
tarnish
these days of hot milk

and fire
that turns into tongues

and tomorrow
that believe in the virtue
of song

you hand him
your pen

because words are necessary
to crack up with pleasure

words for his eyes
brighter than a sea morning
and sand castles

and books that spit
the harmless fire
of dragons

it is time for evening grace

and still have so many
sheep to count

you start to count
one two three

the child in your arms

you need a vertical math table
to contain the grief

a drawbridge
and impossible islands

and a ladder
that rises beyond the flames

life should be more than
hell

you too were once
a child of words

cast
against the wind

you forget the fields
that lit up
like petroleum

and the children
that ran with their shadows

so naked we notice their skulls

deep in their eyes
by the thousands

one war is all it takes
to turn the world upside down

these stories
of blood and daggers

carry back to the caves
where you hid your children

the child already sees
the terror

when evening touches
the threshold of night

faces are disfigured
by long teeth

like in
irrevocable cities

where you stroll
certain mornings

music hullabaloo
motor cars, horns
voices blazing under the sun

in front of banks
like oases

bleached
at gunpoint

life too is a crime
in smile and tie

rushing every day
to and fro and about

luckily in the city
there are museums

as spacious as cathedrals
and with Madonnas

with tears of marble

dropping onto sons
who succumbed
in the hands of executioners

mothers have no idea
what sort of violence
kills their child

mothers have faith

mothers will disguise
reality
to forget their fears

when they see blood
splattered on the walls
of museums

by their crucified sons

you hand a red crayon
to the child
beside you

red light, trucks
and sirens

picking up speed
history and the brain

the idea is to draw
fresh jets of water

cats rising
nine times from their ashes

night of clenched fists
into which young boys
dive

just when you lend
your voice
to animals

glad to put despair
to sleep

you are human
and all humans seek is
a safe haven

such as the phrases you heard
as a child
about the abc of art

if you no longer see
Auschwitz presented
as still life

under the unbearably blue
sky

blue is unbearable
once it betrays
your memory

what remains of Auschwitz
is the setting
for a suburb

small, perfect brick
dwellings

like those days
of young naivete

and bed sheets on clotheslines
swaying
in the gentle breeze

and women sporting spotless
aprons

which they paraded
in front of their children

you too were born
to such everyday cleanliness

white bread
sliced by machines

that cut
your finger

but no one
home was killed
by hatred gone off ground

the day rushed through your veins
like verbs
in the future tense

because the future is a question
young girls asked themselves

when they played
with young boys

a way to distinguish
the best from the blood
on their thighs or flags

the future is now
a question
with multiple answers

like urban noise
disrupting your morning
reading

but you review
in silence
the suffering shapes

that never stop to torment
the chalky lighting
in museums

some mornings you let
the child
play with his flashes in the pan

as you step out
alone

to look in
Francis Bacon's apocalypses
for what went wrong

II

We no longer have faith in this earth
whose womb is filled with dead bodies
its quakes   its tornados   its black ice
its tall trees from which children
hang
Geneviève Amyot

And you continue to write
your poem

with the same hand, the same
world, the same shit
spread over the page

the awkward left hand
when shaking the matter
that does not concern it

except diagonally
seen from shame's perspective

as though it were the hand
of a soldier following
orders

lips stitched, badge stitched
where once the heart was

but here you are

left hand
gentle

with the child and the story
of young Moses
saved from drowning

morning at times is the goodness
from books

with a princess opening her eyes
on a crib
floating adrift down the river

morning is the crazy need
to tell stories of

women giving birth
in the blink
of an eye

simple storytelling
in your mother tongue

a rush, suddenly
a soul

a love you notice
in the astonished hand

opening over swaddling clothes
and soiled
tears

there are mornings
made for loving

and you want to tell them
to this child beside you

like the troubadours of the past
who travelled from town to town

sprinkling
decency
on the war-ravaged

you would like to belong
to the family of conscious
dreamers

who have always
consoled

the world's sequel

and in the morning
you stir awake
the books of holiness

for the child
beside you

though you no longer understand
your world

not its exhausting rush
not its dissonance
in colour

on the giant screens
hanging from buildings

asleep
in time's square

where some men
and women

like you
speechless stare at themselves

in Francis Bacon's
crucified gaze

because this world is no temple

the world is a museum
without walls

in which fire and blood
were used to exterminate
people and angels

still the tiniest of sparrows
is all it takes for a child
to fashion wings for himself

and when the church bell resounds
on Sunday you wonder

if this is piety or a lie

to purse your lips
tightly
in grief

on Sunday you make a vow
with beauty

as you rock
seas and wonders

and your voice
running over the page

as you run
after the child
just to hear him laugh

the child is a mountain lake
deeper
than your fear

and you ready yourself
and dip your faith

in these black
waters protecting
the memory of rock

large tombstones
engravings on fossils

which you resurrect
for the child beside you

his journey is long
and you believe
in miracles

like you this child
was born to a people with wings

that flew across the endless
sky and floods

and you look at him
standing now

in this story
doomed from the start

and you cross
over his chest
your awkward arms

and thankfully you still have
arms

caress, cloud
that you weave
under his tiny footsteps

you, evening spider

the little busy beast
always ready to catch
the monsters under the bed

life in the evening
is a struggle to end
in the warmth of a room

with kisses
on the forehead

and another night
on the watch

you shut the door quietly
to sleep

taking stock of
the day

images blossoming behind thorns
you pull one by one
nonstop

images you planted
near the sunflowers
their heads turned to the noon sun

a garden of youth
is needed to shake up
the present

with its life fire, its smoke
spiralling up
above the firs and maples

the landscape fast asleep
its peace fragile

detecting
the odour of death
rising from the ovens

here you are again
disfigured

like a Francis Bacon
body

blood red, crucifixion
red

you repeat words
that should rectify
the night

night is a book
you read
between the lines

dreams
you can still dream

all you need to do is dig
a narrow passageway in the dark

a cave in which you light
candles
for offerings

a tiny sparkle that encourages
the shadows to waltz

yes, this is all you need

even if there is no orchestra
night alone suffices

and you find
your place
among the animals

created with a handful of clay
and a few ribs

you mould your pride
into a ball
on the wooden floor

as the child screams for you
from the depths of a nightmare

a monster
is attacking him

its mouth
the shape of a scream
in a Francis Bacon painting

this child is a child
of this century

playing massacre
dropping out of the red
of his eyes

this child knows nothing of gods
capable of giving birth
with clay

nothing of the heart
of the world on fire

like the world spinning
around the yellow stars
of Auschwitz and Birkenau

overcoats small, dresses
moth-ridden, a milk bottle
that once belonged to a child

much like the child
falling back asleep
in your skinny arms

night is at times a child
hanging onto the warmth
of a woman

her voice
at risk
in the horizon of darkness

voice of an angel with wings
flattened by fear

you go back to
your own childhood

with its species
that no one threatened

a school, a home
a church

erected at the crossroads
of innocence

where you walked your soul
like a carefree dog

before, way before this barely
visible crack
in the wall of your day

opened
millimetre by millimetre
into the hell awaiting you

on your crinoline dress
like that of your doll

and there
a ghostly odour
stuck in your throat

there like a window
one has broken, an iron
curtain

the sun switched off

and your charred
gaze

there where
you lose it all

words in free fall
into images

fields, camps, corpses
bodies torn to pieces

you, your body of grief
which you slip into a dress
one day nonchalantly

unaware of the fact
it would never
abandon you

even with this child
in your arms

singing like a mockingbird

a bear sleeping
in the forest
of his bed sheets

all this happiness
reinvented
morning and evening

grief is a cancer
gnawing at you
until its final victory

a jail without a jailer

and there in the mirror
you lower your
mother-wolf eyes

night and day
nibbling
on the bars of captivity

you are a prisoner
for empty eyes

darting at you
with a stare that will not forgive

as though you were sentenced
to death

in the arms
of all those dying

as you wander
about in your sentences

chasing after the thousands
of black insects
gathered on the ridge of words

hoping to fall on
a grave
in this eternity of grief

there is a child
beside you

who makes
the language of farms
gleam with joy

that he carries
on his miniature train

and for a second
a word is solidly anchored
in his mouth

pudgy mouth, full mouth
capable of forgetting
red disasters

undoubtedly this is the present

the method is concrete
an impressive imitation of a fair

merry-go-rounds and fanfares
illustrated dictionaries

you believe we can learn
more from circus people

than from the suburban sun
hanging from school windows

life goes on everywhere

even without God
life is an oath

you stammer
when the morning
awakes you

some days the tiniest
of adverbs

rubbing against the adjectives
"good" and "loving"

helps raise
the dough of everyday life

the child beside you
becomes an ogre

as some children do
in the morning

while you scrimp and save
like a squirrel

and prepare lunch
in the blind-spot
of distress

so goes life
and remembrance

when women perform
mistake-free gestures

for children sitting at the table
of common life

waiting for communion

as you go about chasing
after the memories of the apostles

invited one last time
around blood

and flesh becomes
Francis Bacon red

like in Francis Bacon
a tale of torture and resurrection
is giving birth to you

and is served to you
each morning
by nuns in heavy dresses

a crucifix
swaying over their breasts

you were a student
in the devil's shadow

long before you were taught
to pronounce the word "hell"

still burning
beneath the impossible consonants
of its name

III

All things of grace and beauty such that one holds them to one's heart have a common provenance in pain. Their birth in grief and ashes.

Cormac McCarthy,
The Road

This is how your poem
stands up against you

as you stand up
against

simple
piety of simple things

because you are no priestess

but a woman
of troubled night
and libraries

which quiver when attacked
by dust mites

regardless of the rumoured
wisdom of books

you're incapable of
destroying grief

grief is this heart worm
inside you

there, in the tamed
hollow of childhood

like a dot on the Map
of Tendre

a village buried
in ruins

where the catastrophe
left no witness

no story, no face

your memory is a white
patch on the white background

a painting
terribly abstract

a repenting
your fingernails dig into

down to the blood
of words

because words too leave
splinters
in the flesh

when fingers touch
the dead wood
of language

and the ghosts sleeping there
from the beginning of time

your grief
is that ancient

it rises from the silence
of sunken
continents

like ships we believed lost
at the bottom of the abyss

when Earth
was as flat as a penny

your grief does not haul you in

grief can't be exchanged
for some rare commodity

grief is not a perishable fruit

grief follows a path
parallel to yours
and the child's

who does not wish to learn
the arithmetic
of death

the child opens
the window
in his chest

revealing
the horizon of courage

of creatures that meet
and multiply

under the ravenous gaze
of predators

the child wants
no grief instilled
within

for grief makes its way
into your cells
with its cold light

you try to contain grief
by covering it
with silken bed sheets

or with willpower
each time nascent
each time surviving

because grief feels pity
for no one and grief

stands before you
with a gun in its fist

and aims
at the heartbeat of love

grief leads you astray
punctures your eyes
and soul

but the sun is too lonesome
to keep you warm

you try to recall
where it is you lived

before this straw house
you built with your sweat
and hands

yet a straw house
is still
a home

where you can trip
over love

love moves in the shadow
of a word

you hold close to your chest
protectively

when you cannot
feel love

like the touch
of the child beside you

who knows how to make
ocean silence
of forests sing at night

when trees undo
in their braids
for the sunrise

night, a child's only
touch

can outsmart
the world and its grief
be it for a second

you then lead your soul
to the lightning of words

and you forget
the never-ending list
of funeral pyres

kindled by fingers
we considered human

as though you could still
call forth the innocence
within

be it for a second
a fragile second

hanging on some idea
that it might still be time
for the impossible

life that would catch
the naked July wind

against all odds
all tears kept behind
eyes

and cages
within cages within frames
of Francis Bacon's paintings

a small distraction
is all you have
of reason

distraction you repeat
and not forgetfulness

soon your eyes will drown
in the pollution of images

blackened
escaping from a sentence
scribbled sideways

you know your cute naivete
it is sleeping
in a stuffy catechism

which taught you
about fallen angels

then you learned about
your birth rights

in this species
ready to murder

with such pleasure
from which the poem gets written

the child's hand
on your arm

carrying the undersized
clothes from Auschwitz

and the broken baby bottles

and the broken hearts of mothers
wandering back to the garden
of the first woman

and you wonder
how to walk
with this grief

which drags
behind your feet

you, the exiled woman
of the great orchard

you who are looking for an answer
never to be found

what haven will free
the child beside you

what water will quench your thirst
and words

stuck in old-fashioned
metaphors

what heritage of poverty
to hand over

and you continue to walk forward
through your language

more exhausted
than a plough horse

with the dream that this child
will one day pull out a sentence
with his tiny fingers

and will pitch it
with all his calm strength

like he throws
a crystal ball
from the Christmas tree

what is needed is
the reverence of birth
under the trees

cut down from their life
in the past

dying to light up
the darkest syllables
of December

what is needed is a future
with the roughness of fiction
to rough it out

like in those scratchy films
projected
in church basements

in which the word "end"
justified all sacrifice

ready to sacrifice
you too, you would

if you could burn
every shroud

but little ghosts
constantly come back
to people your nights

with their screams
provoking earthquakes

disheartened
you watch
your house fall to pieces

with ideas of the present
built on a handful of books

like a draught
inside your head

exercise at living
among the corpses

luckily there are
books

you can carry
in school yards

where you bit into apples

and learned lessons
on good and evil

where you embraced
all those
old wives' tales

about young girls
red blood, red
sacrifice

horror red

like the howl
feeding bottles let out
under boots

and you see popes
sitting guilt-free
in the paintings by Francis Bacon

this morning's silent
sun

as you make your way
along the tortuous walls
of grief

not understanding why there is
a monstrous hammering inside your
head

yet you hold
tightly on to
the light from nowhere

because a man is a man
though he wears a pope's garment

even if presented as innocent
in the prudish theatrics
of a painting

and you continue to move on
unaware of how much time
is needed to lower your eyelids

before you notice
behind forgiveness

the shadows
of submitted people

like trees
bent over
after a storm

complaining flows
through your veins

as you follow the path
which the child unrolls everyday
up to your heart

wax crayons
bought by the dozen

tracing on paper
a hand
for touching

touching, in spite of yourself
you turn around
to that word that carries you

like a whirlwind of voices
in the sweet wind
night of lanterns

caress, light touch
fingers waltzing

on the hem
of wounds sown
and sown again

in a dignity
we sometimes call a "poem"

happiness held by an invisible
thread

happiness is yours
only if you free it
from this mouth

opened as a howl
setting the sky on fire

Francis Bacon red

yet the child beside you
and his lips

ready to sing
the night

for the glory of images

at your ten fingertips
there are dreams
running like lizards on walls

like Easter
water

the idea is to move
your hand among the images
of shame

tracing those paths
to the sun

the child
knows nothing of the blood
in the chalice

the child is a golden thirst
that splatters against the landscape

the child pulls you, forces you
to walk

into his hallucinations
of the future and space

the child is greater
than the arms
of crucifixions

and you shrinking to being
a girl crying much
in order to love much

you, now the young
and older woman
whose heart folds over

what you see
has no echo

like a grammar gone berserk

a church with cherubs
nailed
by the whiteness of wings

a glass cage
for the prestige of popes

who knew
how to set up hell

what you see every day
rips
through your eye's skin

yet you keep walking
behind the child
your path stationary

you hope that touching
the innocence of grass
we consider weeds

one second of wisdom

like a well
to drop your grief in

up to a water
quivering with beauty

you cover your shoulders
with this nothingness

that looks like a sunrise
of snow

as you contemplate
the morning
dizzy with silence

in the dew on your hands
with the reflection of the world

suddenly masterful
at building the day

you suddenly
become the craftswoman of a shroud

for the souls
beneath the ashes

as though living meant
the work of woman
and modesty

rekindled
with every sparkle
of light

you organize words
under your eyelids

so that the child
beside you

can learn how to climb
the stairs to his dreams

this child is by himself
humanity

this child is a gift
you were not expecting

IV

Till the end, remove shackles,
though your hands be shackled.
Philippe Jaccottet

And you want to learn
to dance

on the charred rope
of words

here you are sheer will power
sheer goal, violent
determination

soaring
like an arrow

or love
too vast for you

here you are
ready to dance
beyond your fears

blinded and deaf
to the cracking in every sky

that collapsed
as soon as you knew how to read

you will never stop learning
from books and from their red
lessons

never forget
the blood that gave birth to you

you were born of anonymous
bayonets

that gashed the flesh
of women and flags

like this soiled
language
you cart in your veins

you are humain
and you know it

you are earth and will go back
to earth

composting
dead bodies
like table leftovers

with stomping of boots
and prayer

a dead body is a dead body

even the child
they care for

as they gas
up the ovens

even the woman
whose milk has soured

who has no one
to breast-feed

from soil to soil
the bark is one
porous like bone

in the evening when you sit
by a lamp

you, sheer will power
sheer desire for lightness
and dancing

because the child
beside you
likes to dance

his muscles stretching
for the magic of modernity

and the geniuses able to transform
a city
into a mushroom of fire

to dance, perhaps
to simply balance

dreams twirling
down into
sleep

after you miss
the beat that rhymes
with each jump by your shadow

you are not a woman
one tosses aside

you, sheer desire
sheer passion for space
and future

you are dancing
the child against your breast

you are dancing
till the day
becomes dizziness

you are dancing a dance
that is proof
of faith

well organized charity

plea of plants
waiting
in the flower shop

a few ounces of water
to welcome the petals

you believe this is
a time
for comforting

the inconsolable flesh
of this grief

you have not been able
to place
in you

if not as a fault
reborn with each birthing

like a calling
surging from the ancestral
earth

as it vomits
its bowels

grief is a volcano
partially extinct

that shakes you
up to anger

and you no longer recognize
the lava
flowing out of your heart gone mad

anger is energy

despair for love
concealed in grief

and you are dancing with the child
in your arms

you keep dancing
wanting to exhaust
the praying voice within

always tempted
by the prediction of powder
and cannons

you have as many
synonyms for misfortune

as you do for the reflection
in rivers

that carry their waters
to the sea
unaware of catastrophe

you say "catastrophe"
as a never-ending
oil spill

that you have to clean
before your legs
are swallowed by darkness

catastrophe, as we sink
like birds

into the comfortable
evening living-room
sofas

you are dancing
to stir
this emotion

you call "grief," "anger"
or "love"

as soon as you find the time
to lift the hurting

and see
the gardens of synonyms

where you have put
the urns of the unknown

your skin is ashen-grey
like a desecrated
cemetery

beast escaped
from prehistory

rushing
towards extinction

but this child
beside you and love

this child and you are dancing
the immemorial journey
from which you emerge

skull still stained
with the blood of women

screaming, making them
want to tear their hearts out

this child and you start
to walk towards grief

cradling this grief like a fever
you have to get rid of
before it gets rid of you

you pull it away
slowly from the suffering
without a face

here you are resolved
to weep your grief

resolved to cherish grief
in mountains

of bones once more
become dust

like smoke that sticks on
and imprisons
cities

you love grief that yells
like a lamb
whose throat is slit

under the Easter gaze
of popes

screams of terrified
nurslings

like the children in Auschwitz
imprisoned in the darkness
of cattle trucks

you know, you have always
been walking

towards a fate common to
human and beast

but you are dancing
as we would commemorate
the longevity of fields

between two grasshopper
offensives

history is ghastly
and you know it

history is rapacious

history has care neither
for economy of harvesting

nor for children
bound like sheafs
for a last supper

because little matters the flesh
when the stomach lets the knife
glitter

you are not the first dancer
and you know it

cannibal music
keeps echoing
under your feet

under your feet, there is
humankind's blood

ever since human is
human

hearts are
devoured
for their boldness

and silence climbs
into skulls

but morning knocks
repeatedly
at your window

and you turn into the woman
grabbing her ankles

memory
with suction pads

earthworm
sea worm, tapeworm
fluke or filaria

ready to rot
the executioner's fist

you keep dancing in the daytime
until the child in your arms
achieves greatness

his questions already
hurting

and your love
can never find an answer

you have neither advice
to give

nor earth to offer as promise

you are no prophet
and you know it

you're a beggar
of joy

twisted and twisted
like Francis Bacon's
red mouths

a meteorologist
on the look-out

in the eye of the hurricane

powerfully ripping
out trees and dreams

but you will not tip over
and you keep dancing

with butterflies
hidden in your heart

for they found
no other place of safety

and you are strong
enough to welcome

the world
in perpetual mourning

which you carry and cradle
until you die

in spite of your tropical
heart
you have the rhythm it takes

to waltz this child
in the eye of the hurricane

time here
is blue and night
has stars

and you want to glimpse
up

above the walls
inside your eyes

and see the place where
faces are still
faces

and cities where sentences
survive beyond
your lips

there surely exists a syntax
for the language of softness

deep inside
your hurting breath

and beyond
tombstones

where the soil is fragile
and the dead awaken
and their voices

you hear
rising above
the complaints of humankind

like a physics
of pain

a science
memorized

prior to images fading within you

in spite of your tropical heart
you are not old enough

to learn the teachings
of the winds that circle around you

the winds circling
around you dancing

with this child and wild hope
provides answers
to earth's murmurings

the earth waiting for
neither repentance nor prayer

as it returns to cycle
of seed
harvest

and humble water
poured over the spring season

circling as unction oil
on the forehead of the newborn

though frightened a hand
can resuscitate
the flesh of words

smothered
by dust

like a testament
of shadow

that you engraved
on your own flesh

the memory of the dead
needs a home

and memory asks you
for water
and a dance

and you invite it
to waltz with you and the child

drunk with joy
and the twirling

you widen

as you break
the unbreakable walls
of your fear

though the wind
and the volcanoes
might wreak vengeance on you

though you are exhausted

in your arms
there is a child looking into your eyes

even if you are not brave
you become a woman
of courage

a woman of open windows

who lets
the day boil over

you have bones stronger
than you imagined

that have not betrayed you

like you will never betray
this small universe

hanging from your neck
for here is mystery
laughing
begging you

never to stop
the dance

ACKNOWLEDGEMENTS

The translator would like to thank Louise Dupré for her presence and for writing such memorable poetry. Thank you to Elana Wolff for her editorial suggestions. The translator acknowledges the financial support of the Government of Canada through the National Translation Program for offering him a grant to work on this translation. A special thank you to Michael Mirolla and Connie Guzzo-McParland at Guernica Editions for publishing this translation. All my gratitude to Elisabeth Pouyfaucon for opening the windows of our homes.

BOOKS BY LOUISE DUPRÉ

POETRY

La peau familière (1983)
Où (1984)
Chambres (1986)
Quand on a une langue, on peut aller à Rome
(with Normand de Bellefeuille, 1986)
Bonheur (1988)
Noir déjà (1993)
Tout près (1998)
Les mots secrets (2002)
Une écharde sous ton ongle (2004)
Plus haut que les flammes (2010)

FICTION

La memoria (1996)
La Voie lactée (2001)
L'été funambule (2008)

DRAMA

Si Cendrillon pouvait mourir! (collective work, 1980)
Tout comme elle, followed by a dialogue with Brigitte Haentjens (2006)

NON-FICTION

La théorie, un dimanche
(with Louky Bersianik, Nicole Brossard,
Louise Cotnoir, Gail Scott, and France Théoret, 1988)
Stratégies du vertige, Trois poètes : Nicole Brossard,
Madeleine Gagnon, France Théoret (1989)
Sexuation, espace, écriture:
La littérature québécoise en transformation
(edited by Louise Dupré, Jaap Lintvelt, and Janet M. Paterson, 2002)

ARTBOOK

Renoncement
(with six artworks by Jean-Luc Herman, 1995)
Parfois les astres
(with Denise Desautels and Jacques Fournier, 2000)
Le noir, la lumière
(with art works by Chan Ky-Yut, 2002)

TRANSLATIONS

Memoria, translated by Liedewij Hawke (1999)
The Milky Way, translated by Liedewij Hawke (2002)
The Blueness of Light: Selected Poems, translated by Antonio D'Alfonso (2005)
High Wire Summer, translated by Liedewij Hawke (2009)
Just Like Her, translated by Erin Moure (2011)
Theory, a Sunday (with Louky Bersianik, Nicole Brossard, Louise Cotnoir, Gail
Scott and France Théoret), translated by Popahna Brandes, Gail Scott, Nicole
Peyrafitte, Luise von Flottow and Erica Weitzman (2013)

ABOUT THE AUTHOR AND THE TRANSLATOR

Louise Dupré has been active in Quebec as a member of the Académie des lettres du Québec and the Royal Society of Canada. Her work has received numerous awards. In 2011, *Plus haut que les flammes* won the Governor General's Award for poetry as well as the Grand Prix Québecor du Festival International de la Poésie de Trois-Rivières. *Tout comme elle* was produced on stage and directed by Brigitte Haentjens in Toronto in 2011, during the Luminato Festival. Her work has been translated into various languages. Louise Dupré lives in Montreal.

"Louise Dupré has given us an accomplished book that evokes images of concentration camps, the paintings of Francis Bacon, and the love of a child, safeguard of the future, a fragile image of our fundamental survival, in order to avoid total disappearance... A superb book, its intensity so deep that we would like to quote it in its entirety, a perfectly essential book."

Hugues Corriveau, Le Devoir

Antonio D'Alfonso is a writer, an editor, and a filmmaker. His works have been translated and published in numerous languages. In 2005, he won the Trillium Award for his novel, *Un vendredi du mois d'août* (*A Friday in August,* Exile Editions). He lives both in Toronto and Montreal.

"A poet and her grandson climb out of the horrors of the twentieth century. On the ground on which murder spat blood, life blossoms. The narrative track is deceptively simple, the outcome courageously heroic. Few words, troubled images, the fragile rhythm of self-analysis: this is what faith in humankind has become. And yet sparsity reveals grandeur of intent. Louise Dupré's verse is envelopped with grace. *Beyond the Flames* in its original version won the Governor General's Award in 2011. This long poem in four parts stands above many other poetry books. Neither deconstruction, nor lyricism, neither song, nor prayer, this work offers such an inspired revelation that it seems so unique as to form its own genre. A great moment in literature."

Antonio D'Alfonso